MARVIN THE MOST

MARVELOUS MOLE

Words by John Davies

Illustrations by John Davies

First published 2024 by AdJon Books, Port Talbot

For Adrianne – there is no one compares with you

Love and hugs to my fab family

Ian and Tina

Freya, Ayla and Osian

Spider's Domain

Fidipus Adux the spider

Loved messing about on the net

He was quite an expert and even a text-pert

He never broke into a sweat

His fingers flew over the keyboard

In front of his favourite screen

He built his domain without any strain

The finest that you could have seen

He merged art and science so well

Weaving colours with shapes and with form

Each page came alive right on his disc drive

On his internet worldwide platform

With precision he built night and day

A tapestry that shone with delight

A weaver of tales with the wind in his sails

He never stopped once for a byte!

His digital design was a wonder

Right down to its every sound bite

He spun it and wove it and ran it and drove it

For hits on his spider website

Frankie and Carlie

Frankie was a bullfrog with speckles on his back

He sang a soulful song for which he had a knack

He lived beside a sparkling pond with rushes all around

At eve of day he sang away it was a lovely sound

Carlie was a caterpillar so colourful and gay

She crawled through the farmer's fields until the end of day

The sound of singing made her stop beside a sparkling pond

It was such a lovely melody she thought she would respond

Carlie cried, 'Oh, please come out, you sing so tunefully

Frankie hopped out from the pond and said quite truthfully

'It's me that sings, it's me you hear and who are you my dear?'

'My name is Carlie; I've travelled far and I'm very glad I'm here'

Then Carlie said to Frankie, 'I love your voluminous voice'

'Shall we get married tomorrow? I'm sure I've made a good choice'

They discovered a dove in the next field on his leg he had a gold ring

Frankie hopped to that dove and asked, 'Will you sell me that thing?'

The dove was delighted to sell his ring for a silver half a crown

Carlie and Frankie were married that day by a mouse who lived in the town

They dined on potage, crepes and custard the room was filled with laughter

They danced all night by the poolside and lived happily ever after

Disreputable Dog

I have a big brown spotted dog

I got him as a tiny sprog

Sometimes he can be well-behaved

But he can also be depraved

He's good at zoomies, running round

Knocking ornaments to the ground

And when he's out away from home

He'll bark and bark at a garden gnome

When back at home he still annoys

By hiding all the children's toys

He'll also sit and stare at me

And then climb up upon my knee

He'll shadow me right down the hall

Under my feet and make me fall

Runs in the house muddy and wet

What to do with this naughty pet?

He made my face turn really blue

When he ate another dog's poo!

He made me feel quite sick as well

When he released a putrid smell

I have a big brown spotted dog

I've had him from a tiny sprog

Can be quite disreputable

Yet can be quite adorable

The Salmon of Knowledge

Oh, splendid silver salmon

How swift you swim the sea

You cross the ocean calmly

So fleet and fancy free

Your knowledge is expansive

You know the way so well

Do you use your sense of sight

And your sense of smell?

And when you reach the river

The place where you were born

Are you justly joyful

And not at all forlorn?

You've swum the salty water

And now the sparkling stream

But then you realize you're wrong

Lost your way it would seem!

Puppy

Whose puppy's this? I think I know

Its owner's name is Calvin Crow

He's full of joy, his face aglow

I watch him laugh with great gusto

His puppy's name is simply Jake

And Jake loves eating currant cake

He also swims around the lake

And when he's wet, he'll shake and shake

Tired puppy soon falls asleep

Into his mind sweet dreams then creep

His sleep is sound and deep as deep

There was no need for counting sheep

He rises from his comfy bed

With thoughts of breakfast in his head

With stomach full he is well-fed

Another day of fun ahead

Leary Limericks

There once was a young boy who barked

Which made all of his friends feel narked

He would sit up and beg

Then lift his left leg

And leave all the tree trunks well-marked

There once was an old man named Jack

Whose teeth all went clickety clack

And clickety clack

And clickety clack

And clickety clickety clack

There once was a whimsical fairy

Who spent all her days being merry

She whistled and sang

Then with a loud bang

Transmuted into a canary

The Flatulent Frog

A friendly frog lost every friend

Because of gas from his back end

He hopped about the boggy ground

Leaving a noxious gas all round

Each hop brought forth a further blight

Leaving faces wrinkled and white

He sat on a log feeling blue

Wishing for friends old and new

His croaking sadness filled the night

His ribbits echoed till daylight

But still his gas just smelled like doom

The friendly frog was filled with gloom

Then one day he met a brave newt

Who proved to be just so astute

Newt knew the lore of nature's ways

And said he'd cure the frog in days

They set off as the sun set low

A gentle breeze blew soft and slow

Carrying the scent of herbs so sweet

The newt said, 'Now you're for a treat'

Herbs that grew in this secret place

Would banish his smell without trace

So frog ate up all that he could

And hoped that they would do him good

He reached his home and slept all night

And rose refreshed in bright sunlight

His noisome odours were dispelled

His rotten gas no longer smelled

He hopped about the boggy ground

With all of his friends gathered round

Atmosphere

Is it air or is it aura, call it what you like

Shimmering sunlight filtering through, even on my mate Mike!

So-called experts have seen changes so they seem to say

Sometimes it's so bright and blue and sometimes dark and grey

Would we rather call it climate, that can also be

Can it have a certain flavour like a cup of tea?

Some places have an ambience that speaks to us out loud

They can also have an odour like a sportsground crowd

You can feel such good vibrations from a certain place

There's no way you could feel that good up in outer space

The aroma in a restaurant is really rather fine

It tempts you to go right on in so you can wine and dine

It cradles the earth in its cuddly hold, unseen yet all around

Dancing with clouds in graceful flight yet keeping them all earthbound

The air about us has its uses please don't ever doubt it

Both you and I and everyone could never live without it!

Marvin the Most Marvelous Mole

Marvin the most marvelous mole

Started digging a deep dark hole

He dug so fast and with great skill

Made a mountain of his mole hill

He travelled down and met a worm

The frightened worm began to squirm

'Please don't eat me,' he protested

Marvin left him un-mole-ested

He dug on down through roots of trees

He could not work his way through these

Stopped to rest, ate some granola

Drank a drop of coca-mole-a

Deeper and deeper he dug down

Working harder without a frown

Getting hungry digging this hole

Had a small snack of guaca-mole

Dug right down to he knew not where

And then he broke into fresh air

Didn't bother with regalia

Even though he'd found Australia!

The Happy Spirit

Ghostly wraiths and ghoulish spectres

Roam the realm of darkest night

This happy spirit full of fun

Haunts homes, but not to give fright

In tattered robes with hat on head

And some mischief on his mind

He plays his pranks without a word

But never to be unkind

He floats through walls with ghostly grace

And makes the living quiver

They would wonder, 'Is someone there?'

Looking round with a shiver

His tricks were many and such fun

Like rattling pots and pans

Scraping a chair and hiding keys

Are all just part of his plans

Don't be afraid, this ghost is kind

Entertainment is his goal

If you sense a presence unseen

Don't fret, he is a friendly soul!

The Jester

So silly and wacky such a real buffoon

Just cuckoo and kooky a japester and goon

Bizarro and bozo his antics are wild

With a jest and a jibe his jokes never mild

His clothes are a riot a colourful mess

Patchwork and polka dots and even a dress

He starts with some silliness then adds the absurd

Telling tales and jokes that no one has heard

From noble to peasant no target too grand

He mocks king and queen then does a handstand

His mirthful blue eyes just twinkle with glee

As he joyfully performs his wisecracking spree

A jocular jokist spreading laughter around

His tricks and his jesting really astound

With humour and wit, he claims his great worth

A magical madcap and master of mirth

Leary Limericks

There once was a lady called Kate

Who always turned up rather late

She missed all the buses

And caused lots of fusses

And married a man called Jess Waite

There once was a lady from Noredum

Who suffered from terrible boredom

She went for a ride

On a rickety slide

And slid off the slide with a sore bum

There was a young lady called Polly

Who couldn't quite open her brolly

She gave it a clout

Then started to shout

'I hate this old brolly, by golly!'

The Strange Story of the Cow and the Moon

Hey diddle diddle the dog played the fiddle

The cow leaped up to the moon

The little lamb laughed to see such a stunt

And the cow took a dish and a spoon

So where did she go did, she fly high or low?

She went to a lunar tea party

The hot cross buns were two for a penny

And the pies there were really quite hearty

The kettle was steaming the dormouse was dreaming

And the party had tables well laid

Mad hatter was there white rabbit as well

And the queen of hearts dressed in brocade

Little Jack Dorner sat in the corner

Watching a twinkling star

Down came a spider and sat on his knee

And started to play a sitar

Good Doctor Koster who came from West Gloster

Danced round a mulberry bush

Three blind mice squeaked ever so loud

The good doctor told them to shwsh

The party was over for this cow called Clover

She picked up her dish and her spoon

The little lamb laughed while packing her bag

It was time to return from the moon

I'd Rather Be

What would I rather be, if I couldn't be me?

I'd rather be an owl in flight

With eyes as big as saucers

But then owls just come out in the night

Perhaps I'd rather be a river

Ever changing, running free

With pure water swiftly flowing

But then I'd end up in the sea

Perhaps I'd rather be a penguin

In my black and white suit, I'd look really nice

I'd slide and glide on my belly bright

But penguins live in snow and ice

Perhaps I'd rather be a tree

With new green leaves about to sprout

And branches swaying, my roots down deep

But trees don't ever move about

Perhaps I'd rather be a scarecrow

To scare the crows with my ghastly glare

Standing proudly in a farmer's field

But scarecrows just don't go anywhere

What would I rather be, if I couldn't be me?

An owl, a river or perhaps a bee

A penguin, scarecrow or perhaps a tree?

I think, perhaps, I'd just rather be me!

Mars Odyssey

Fidipus Adux the spider

Took a trip right up to the stars

He shot off in a ship with a light-hearted quip

And landed quite safely on Mars

He thought that the Martians looked freaky

With long noses and big bright black eyes

Antennae that twirled, red hair that was curled

And walking on four legs crabwise

In glorious gardens they grew

Red veggies and red apple trees

And planted in tubs were red pepper shrubs

Which made poor old Fidipus sneeze

In the garden perched up on the trees

Was a glider, just like a huge bee

The Martians said gliders live only on spiders

So Fidipus decided to flee

He raced then right back to his ship

And made up his mind not to roam

The universe wide without a good guide

He felt he was safer at home!

Things I'm Really Good At

Let me tell you of the things that I do so well

I'm a master of many things, but my head won't swell

In a world of talents, mine shine really bright

Even though not everything seems to go quite right

When I meet someone new and he says his name

I forget it within minutes much to my great shame

I go shopping for my food and store it on that day

Three weeks later it's gone off so I throw it all away

Master chef in the kitchen, I can cook most anything

The problem is that I burn almost everything

I can even burn tap water it's really easy for me

It's a skill that I possess, it comes so naturally

But my very special skill is losing my car keys

The keys are so elusive, they vanish with great ease

When I pick up vases with my clumsy mitts

They sometimes slip and fall and smash in little bits

My timing is amazing, really, really grand

I never ever can arrive at the time I planned

I'm very careful planting lots of flower seeds

But all that seems to grow are lots and lots of weeds

Let me tell you of the things that I'm really good at

Master of most anything, there's no denying that

In a world of talents, mine shine really bright

But sometimes, only sometimes, things don't work out right!

Leary Limericks

There was a young man from Devizes

Whose ears were of different sizes

The left one was small

Couldn't see it at all

The right one won prizes for sizes

There was a young man name of Broad

Who prodded a tiger called Maud

She pounced on him quickly

With claws long and prickly

Now he's called by his friends Mister Claude

There was an old woman from Droop

Who only ate hot chicken soup

Started clucking one day

Laid eggs in the hay

And moved from her house to a coop

Poppy and Percy

Poppy the pig lived on a farm

Plumpish and pink and full of charm

Proudly she pranced round her domain

Picking up peelings in the rain

Puddles were where she loved to play

Prancing and splashing through the day

Pally with all the creatures there

Pretty fond of the old brown mare

Percy peacock with feathers fine

Paraded about - how they'd shine

Pacing round he put on a show

Preening his feathers like a beau

Pig and peacock, such an odd pair

Perfect partners without a care

Proud to be friends they loved to dance

Perchance they would chance a romance

Poppy and Percy having fun

Played on the farm in the bright sun

Pleased to be such good company

Prepared for a life full of glee

New Boots and Underpants

I'm very proud of my new brown boots

They're made of leather, so soft to touch

With twirling laces, they feel so light

And with every step I love them so much

I'm also proud of my new underpants

They hold me snug in a warm embrace

Made of cotton and really comfy

They really put a smile on my face

Boots and underpants, a perfect pair

Worn together they make my heart sing

Only trouble is – I'm locked outside

And I don't have on another thing!

In the Jungle

In the jungle where the trees are tall

Lives a monkey who is naughty and small

He swings through the trees causing trouble

Then he dashes away at the double

He'll eat a banana and throw down the peel

Then loudly laugh when his friends slip and squeal

He'll hide in bushes and jump out with glee

To frighten his friends like a wild banshee

In the jungle where the trees are small

Lives a brown bear whose tales are tall

With mischievous grin he tells mammoth lies

And the rest of the animals just roll their eyes

He claimed he caught a whopping great whale

And he could fly when he spun his short tail

He once beat a cheetah in a road race

And flew in a rocket to outer space

This story has now come to its end

Hope you believe it my very good friend

For would I tell you a bear-faced lie?

There's no monkey business from this guy!

Peter Lee

There was a boy called Peter Lee

Who plotted pranks with greatest glee

He tricked his friends and made them sigh

With mischievous glint in his eye

From dawn till dusk, he'd plot and scheme

To make one and all jump and scream

No one was safe from Peter's wit

Even the mayor once fell for it

Placed a whoopee pad on a chair

Laughed when teacher jumped in the air

Hid quietly behind a door

Jumped out then laughed when Daddy swore

Plastic spider in sister's bag

Giggled to see her scream and gag

In Dad's mower, a rubber snake

Screamed with laughter to see him quake

One day his laughter turned to cries

Pranks were returned to his surprise

Tripped because his laces were tied

Salt in his tea dented his pride

Policeman calling at his house

Tape beneath his computer mouse

Now his days of pranks are ended

Learned his lesson, ways are mended!

Lucky Pants

I have a pair of underpants

They always bring me luck

They're a really brilliant shade of red

Just like a fire truck

One day I went out fishing

I had my red pants on

I thought my luck was really in

But all the fish had gone

I went to watch my football team

Red pants newly washed

Not a lucky day at all

My team got really squashed

We had a test in school today

I thought I had it nailed

Even with my red pants on

I didn't pass, I failed

I wore my lucky underpants

To bid for a stamp online

I did my best with my best bid

But another bid beat mine

My lucky underpants don't work

Even when they're clean

I'm going to throw them in the bin

And try a pair of green!

Leary Limericks

There once was a great swarm of bees

Who performed aerial tricks on the breeze

Flew a figure of eight

Flew up, down then straight

And thought they were just the bee's knees

The limerick's a very fine bird

The funniest rhyme that you've heard

It has a great beak

From which it will squeak

Some words that are really absurd

There was a young poet named Prime

Could not get his poems to rhyme

Every word that he tried

Didn't work at all

But he refused to give up writing

Chips

Oh, the joy of eating chips

The taste of vinegar on my lips

I put a little salt on too

But don't expect me to share with you!

Chips are scrumptious, chips are great

Sometimes I eat them on a plate

Chips just bring such joy to me

But how I wish they were fat-free

Maris Piper's play their part

King Edward's are the a la carte

But chips are full of fat it seems

And fat-free chips lie in my dreams

So, here's to chips – fat and all

They simply hold me in their thrall

Fat-free chips are just a dream

Real chips just reign supreme!

Boring Ben

There was a boy called Boring Ben

He sometimes laughed – just now and then

His friends all thought him such a bore

He was always home by half past four

Ben was such a tidy guy

He always wore a shirt and tie

His hands were never, ever dirty

He never would be mad or shirty

Questioned in class by mister Salter

Ben's reply would flit and falter

At sports he was a hopeless case

He'd trip and fall flat on his face

At exams he would not flop

But never bottom, never top

He never caused a wild uproar

His schoolmates called him Ben the Bore

But deep inside a fire burned

When danger threatened Ben soon turned

You've guessed by now, don't need to be told

He's the Superhero – Ben the Bold!

Stones

In streams and fields where flowers sway

Stones are lying from here to Bombay

Stones are scattered all around

Upon the earth and in the ground

Stones are tough, stones are hard

Stones can be quite avant garde

They tend to lie where they belong

They're sometimes round and sometimes long

Stones are patient and very wise

They're never angry and don't tell lies

Some hold secrets that they will keep

While others simply seem to sleep

Stones are funny, stones are great

They don't get tired, they're never late

In water big stones just go plop

Flat ones skip along then stop

Stones are steadfast, stones are staid

Your faith in stones will never fade

Stones will never moan or groan

You're never alone with a trusty stone!

Veronica

Veronica was young and so sweet

She frolicked and played without care

She did not mind snow and sleet

And she wasn't so easy to scare

She walked with a waddling gait

Serene in her tuxedo suit

Fresh fish was all that she ate

And her sense of smell was astute

She loved to slide on her belly

Wherever she found some ice

Her breath was sometimes smelly

But her boyfriend thought that quite nice

Now, you think that I'm telling a tale

With a face that's fixed in a grin

But this story is not a folktale

Veronica is a penguin!

A Lesson Learned

Fidipus Adux the spider

Was eager to buy himself shoes

But he thought it unfair, he needed four pair

And he couldn't afford Jimmy Choos

Fidi then searched all around

He asked all the birds and the bees

A clever old crow then told him to go

To the woods where the shoes grow on trees

Fidi travelled all day and all night

Until he arrived at the place

He picked pairs of red stitched with gold thread

And walked off with pride and with grace

Fidi's heart sang with joy and delight

He started for home with great glee

He hopped and he skipped and never once tripped

And he got home in time for his tea

Then he got a quite nasty surprise

His shoes wouldn't grip his home web

He fell to the ground saw stars all around

His high spirits soon started to ebb

Fidi took off his lovely new shoes

His stomach turned over and churned

'It's better by far to stay as you are'

Was the lesson that Fidi had learned

Leary Limericks

There was a young boy from Alsace

Who wanted to cross a crevasse

He slipped on some moss

And half way across

He fell right onto his bottom

A giant fell off a high wall

He bounced off the floor like a ball

Each bounce made him shorter

By a foot and a quarter

Until he was just two feet tall

There once was a school on a hill

Whose pupils could never sit still

They would fidget and twitch

And scratch at an itch

Cos the school was built on an anthill

Locked Out

Oh me, oh my, how can it be?

I've locked myself out; oh, silly me!

I've searched my pockets hoping to find

The keys that I know I've left behind

I'm trapped outside alone and blue

And I really don't know what to do

I rattle the door and bang like mad

It wouldn't budge which makes me sad

In the garden I find some wire

Doesn't work, I start to perspire

I try the windows all around

Not an open one to be found

I plead with the door to let me in

But the door stays closed and seems to grin!

Alas my efforts are all in vain

And then, by golly, it starts to rain

I quickly dash around the house

To shelter in the old greenhouse

I sit and wait for the rain to stop

Until the last drip goes ker-plop

I stroll up to the kitchen door

Should I have tried this door before?

I tried the door and was I shocked?

It opened up, it wasn't locked!

Football

I am a leather football full of air and round

I sometimes fly up through the air then roll along the ground

I'm kicked around then headed and even sometimes caught

Through many games of football which really are hard-fought

I sometimes get excited when the crowds all shout and scream

I bounce up so much higher and float as in a dream

Sometimes when it's raining and I've got a coat of mud

It's very hard to bounce along I simply slip and scud

I'm scuffed and scarred but bounce on still

And love when players dribble dodging with great skill

There are some wacky moments with some wayward shots

And even big stars missing from the penalty spots!

I've seen it all, the victory sweet

The disappointment in sad defeat

So, you can kick me high or pass me low

Football forever! I'm the star of the show!

Impulsive

I sometimes act upon a whim

The things I do can be quite dim

Some things I've done just make me cringe

I shrug my shoulders and don't whinge

The things I did still make me blink

Like when I dyed my hair bright pink

I jumped in the sea for a dare

Came out with seaweed in my hair

'Get a tattoo', said my best chum

So went and got one on my bum

You might think I'm quite a chump

Doing a sky-high bungee jump

Love to sing at karaoke

Even though my voice is croaky

Should have given much more thought to

Saying things I shouldn't ought to

I sometimes act just on a whim

And things I do can be quite dim

But no regrets for what I've done

I live a life that's full of fun!

Paddy the Pygmy Goat

Young Paddy was a pygmy goat

With a black and white spotted coat

His legs were short, his horns were curled

He longed to see more of the world

He left the farm one sunny day

Heading for Old Botany Bay

He thought it was just down the road

So like a soldier off he strode

A whirlwind took him by surprise

And lifted him into the skies

He landed many miles away

Right on a busy motorway

The traffic whizzed by to and fro

He didn't know which way to go

A kindly rabbit then popped out

Tried hard to speak but had to shout

'Just follow me right down this hole

It's very safe and we can stroll'

The cars went thundering overhead

As through the tunnel they both sped

They came out in a farmer's field

Just where a fox lay quite concealed

The fox jumped out, gave them a fright

Rabbit and goat were put to flight

His little legs moved oh so fast

He lost his breath and stopped at last

He wished he'd never gone away

Just stayed at home and played all day

A whirlwind took him by surprise

And lifted him into the skies

His story soon became folklore

But Paddy left his home no more!

Katie the Cow

Katie the cow was quite young and lean

With an allergy to grass and all things green

She lived in the barn both night and day

All she could eat was boring old hay

If she ate grass her nose would soon twitch

She would sneeze and cough and her eyes would itch

No lush pastures in which she could graze

And no sunlit meadows on bright sunny days

The wise old bull paid a visit to Kate

And saw straight away that she was distrait

He said, 'There's a woman who lives in the wood

At spells and potions, she is very good'

The very next day Kate walked all the way

And found the old woman, whose hair was grey

She told the old woman of her sad plight

The old woman said, 'We'll soon put you right'

She mixed up a potion of roots and a herb

And when it was boiling the smell was superb

Katie drank all of it to the last drop

Thanked the old woman and ran home non-stop

The very next morning she rose with the dawn

To find that her allergy had faded and gone

No more sneezing or coughing or tears

Katie could graze in the fields with no fears!

Leary Limericks

Experiments can sometimes go wrong

And they also can cause quite a pong

A cloud of brown smoke

Made everyone choke

And it made people cough in Hong Kong

There was an old man from New Delhi

On each foot he wore an old welly

He felt such a toff

But when they came off

His feet were so terribly smelly

There once was a man from Dundee

Who trawled in the wide-open sea

He was totally thrilled

When his trawl net was filled

But he never had fish for his tea

This Is Not A Stick

I found a stick in the woods and took it home with me

What can I use it for? Anything I want it to be

I am a horseman charging with the Light Brigade

This is not a stick, it is a sharp steel blade

I am a famed musician, a highly paid pop star

This is not a stick, it's my electric guitar

I went fishing on the pier and caught a great big cod

This is not a stick, it's my brand-new fishing rod

I roam around old houses and then I see a spectre

This is not a stick, it's a ghastly ghost detector

I am a wily wizard of casting spells I'm fond

This is not a stick, it is a magical wand

I found a stick in the woods and took it home with me

What can I use it for? Anything I want it to be!

To the Anchovy

Oh, little fish of silver hue

I dedicate this ode to you

A salty snack beyond compare

The chef will serve you up with flair

Your tiny body filled with taste

In any dish or as a paste

In oil or salt you're packed so neat

A tasty treat that's hard to beat

A plate of pasta you will grace

On pizza you have pride of place

Caesar Salad you will flavour

On hot toast a taste to savour

You add the zing, the tang, the zest

That will put hairs upon your chest

But for me you're a big bad dream

For your flavour just makes me scream!

Fantasyland

There is a place called Fantasyland

Where imagination runs wild

And if you ever visit this place

Your mind will become beguiled

You'll see a stairway in the sky

That leads into the clouds

And when you climb it you will see

Fantastic cheering crowds

A tiger which has fairy wings

Will flit from tree to tree

And hopping on one hundred legs

Here comes a giant flea

Rivers flowing back upstream

To their mountain source

Play forever and a day

On a million-hole golf course

All the animals have two tails

And the cats all wear top hats

Lots of cheese just grows on trees

Which pleases the mice and rats

When you feel down think of these things

You'll feel better and start to laugh

It's not just a daydream that you'll have

It's a daydream and a half!

Rumour Has It

They're whispered softly, as tales unfold

They spread like wildfire, uncontrolled

'Rumour has it' people say

And stories snowball day by day

Rumour has it that in the park

Strange things happen after dark

Fountain spouting water bright

Spouts out cola in the night

Baldy teacher with strange glasses

Is thought by all the junior classes

To be an alien from outer space

Sending signals back to base

Rumour has it – I've heard just now

Down on the farm there's a big brown cow

It has horns of gold, a coat of silk

Produces chocolate flavoured milk

The head in my school was really odd

He came from far away Cape Cod

Carried a telescope and a penknife

Must have been a pirate in a previous life

Rumours come and pass around

Rumours come and rumours abound

Take it with a pinch of salt they say

Rumour has it – could be the truth one day!

Teapot

Oh, lowly teapot, plump and fine

Guardian of the brew divine

With rounded belly, curving spout

You brew the tea; we pour it out

You sit upon the table mat

Wrapped up in your cozy hat

Within your depths the tea is brewing

For extra strength we leave it stewing

You pour the tea so straight and neat

Refreshing brew, a real treat

Fingers wrapped round cup so tight

And lips that sip with such delight

Not just a pot, but our best friend

To one and all a perfect blend

You warm the body and the soul

Much better than a casserole

Oh, lowly teapot it is so true

There is such joy that springs from you

May your handle and your spout

Pour out pleasure and not conk out!

Leary Limericks

There was a young lady called Nellie

Who loved eating lots of green jelly

She'd gobble it down

And never slow down

Now she wobbles from nose down to belly

There once was a pizza so grand

It's toppings were spread out by hand

It looked a delight

With cheese melted right

But it tasted quite totally bland

There once was a snowman called Pat

Who loved to just gossip and chat

He sat by the fire

Began to perspire

And melted all over the mat

Ants in my Pants

I sat on a tuffet like little Miss Muffet

Now an army of ants has invaded my pants

Their tiny feet march to a rhythmic beat

They scurry and roam in my own private home

The royal queen leads the advance

Her loyal army trail in a trance

Forging their way through threads and seams

In single file, in groups and in teams

Their tiny feet tickle against my skin

I scratch and wriggle, twist and spin

They climb and crawl this bustling crew

What can I do? if I only knew

What do they seek in this perilous quest?

Perhaps some crumbs or to make a nest

I whip my pants off, jump in the shower

They all disappear in less than an hour!

Cottage Pie

I'm so confused, now tell me why

There are no cottages in cottage pie

I find it funny and rather droll

There's no toad in toad in the hole

And now I am in great turmoil

There are no babies in baby oil

Now I'm about to make a racket

Does a potato wear a jacket?

I just sit here, so sad and sigh

There are no shepherds in shepherd's pie

I think I'll start a brand-new blog

On why there's no dog in a hot dog

I was asked a question by my mate Sidney

'Why has a kidney bean got no kidney?'

And have you ever even been

Out on a run with a runner bean?

So, you may ask, 'What's in a name?'

Don't ask me – I'm not to blame!

Also by John Davies

Children's picture books
Darren the Dragon, Darren and the Draaken, Darren and Derwyn, Darren and the Duke of
Darkness, Darren and the Drought, Darren's Dilemma, Darren and the Danthralite

Trevor the One-eyed Tractor, Trevor the Tractor to the Rescue

Four Little Guinea Pigs
Tony the Toaster
Garden Party
The Soup Dragon

Poetry for younger readers
How to be a Dog
Antics on the Allotment
The Moustache on the Mantlepiece
The Pearl of Great Price
Every Penny a Prisoner

Short stories for juveniles
Ten Terrific Tales
Ten More Terrific Tales
The Mystery of the Missing Vizsla

For older readers
Hewl - Stori Geraint Griffiths (Welsh language)
Chester to Chepstow – Journal of a Bike Journey
Lyrics and Limericks
100 Years of Port Talbot Harriers, 1921 – 2021
The Leaf That Refused To Fall

Printed in Great Britain
by Amazon